Self-Esteem for Women

Proven Techniques and Habits to Grow Your Self-Esteem, Assertiveness and Confidence in Just 60 Days

By

Maria van Noord

© **Copyright 2018 - All rights reserved.**

The content contained within this book may not be reproduced, duplicated or transmitted without direct written permission from the author or the publisher.

Under no circumstances will any blame or legal responsibility be held against the publisher, or author, for any damages, reparation, or monetary loss due to the information contained within this book. Either directly or indirectly.

Legal Notice:
This book is copyright protected. This book is only for personal use. You cannot amend, distribute, sell, use, quote or paraphrase any part, or the content within this book, without the consent of the author or publisher.

Disclaimer Notice:
Please note the information contained within this document is for educational and entertainment purposes only. All effort has been executed to present accurate, up to date, and reliable, complete information. No warranties of any kind are declared or implied. Readers acknowledge that the author is not engaging in the rendering of legal, financial, medical or professional advice. The content within this book has been derived from various sources. Please consult a licensed professional before attempting any techniques outlined in this book.

By reading this document, the reader agrees that under no circumstances is the author responsible for any losses, direct or indirect, which are incurred as a result of the use of information contained within this document, including, but not limited to, — errors, omissions, or inaccuracies.

Table Of Contents

CHAPTER 1: INTRODUCTION - WHAT IS SELF-ESTEEM? 1

Signs of Low Self-Esteem 2

Signs of High Self-Esteem 4

Why Do Women have Low Self-Esteem? 4

Importance of Self-Esteem 6
   Self-Discovery Questions on Your Current Level of Self-Esteem 7

CHAPTER 2: THE COMPONENTS OF BUILDING SELF-ESTEEM 9

The Practice of Living Consciously 10

The Practice of Self-Acceptance 11

The Practice of Self-Responsibility 12

The Practice of Self-Assertiveness 14

The Practice of Living with a Purpose 15

The Practice of Personal Integrity 17
   Self-Assessment Section 19
   Self-Questions to Gauge Your Present State of Conscious Life 19
   Self-Questions to Gauge Your Present State of Self-Acceptance 19
   Self-Questions to Gauge Your Present State of Self-Responsibility 20
   Self-Questions to Gauge Your Present State of Self-Assertiveness 21
   Self-Questions to Gauge Your Present State of Living Purposefully 21
   Self-Questions to Gauge Your Present State of Personal Integrity 22

CHAPTER 3: HABITS AND HOW TO USE THEM FOR THE GOOD   23

The Cue   24

The Routine   28

The Reward   29

The Importance of Identifying the Habit Loop   29

Replacing Old Bad Habits with New Good Ones   30
   Self-Assessment Questions On Your Current Level of Habits   31

CHAPTER 4: PRACTICAL EXAMPLES   33

The Practice of Living Consciously   33
   NLP Techniques   33
   Affirmations   35
   Visualization   35
   Meditation   35
   Maintaining a Diary   36

The Practice of Self-Acceptance   37
   NLP Techniques   37
   Affirmations   37
   Visualization   38
   Meditation   38
   Maintaining a Diary   38

The Practice of Self-Responsibility   39
   NLP Techniques   39
   Affirmations   40
   Visualization   40
   Meditation   41
   Maintaining a Diary   42

The Practice of Self-Assertiveness   42
   NLP Techniques   42
   Affirmations   43

Visualization	44
Meditation	44
Maintaining a Diary	45

The Practice of Living with Purpose — 46
- NLP Techniques — 46
- Affirmations — 47
- Visualization — 47
- Meditation — 48
- Maintaining a Diary — 49

The Practice of Personal Integrity — 50
- NLP Techniques — 50
- Affirmations — 50
- Visualization — 51
- Meditation — 51
- Maintaining a Diary — 52

CHAPTER 5: WORKBOOK — 53

Workbook for the Practice of Living Consciously — 54
- NLP Techniques – Focus on Your Thoughts — 54
- NLP Techniques – Prayers — 55
- Workbook for the Practice of Self-Acceptance — 58
- Workbook for the Practice of Self-Responsibility — 59
- Workbook for the Practice of Self-Assertiveness — 61
- Workbook for the Practice of Living With Purpose — 63
- Workbook for the Practice of Personal Integrity — 64

CHAPTER 6: CONCLUSION — 67

Chapter 1: Introduction - What is Self-Esteem?

Mary Angelou said, *"Success is liking yourself, liking what you do, and liking how you do it."* You have a high esteem of yourself when you attempt to achieve success in life on your terms.

Ask these questions of yourself:
- Are you proud of yourself?
- Do you like yourself the way you are?
- What are the topmost traits in you that make you proud?

If you are not able to answers these questions confidently or you feel uncomfortable having to answer them, then it is likely that you have low self-esteem. Before understanding why many of us have problems with self-esteem, we need to know the definition of self-esteem.

Self Esteem For Women

So, what is self-esteem? Self-esteem is a reflection of the respect and regard you have for yourself. A woman with a healthy level of self-esteem does not need external factors to feel good about herself. She does not need her husband telling her she looks good or that she is intelligent or that she's a good mother. She does not need her boss to tell her she does a great job at work.
Instead, a woman with a high level of self-esteem is keenly aware of her strengths and weaknesses. She accepts her strengths with pride, her weaknesses with humility, and is confident, assertive, and proud of her capabilities without being arrogant. She understands that she needs to work on her weaknesses and is happy to share the benefits of her strengths with others.

Self-esteem is an essential identity issue that is vital for joy and happiness in our lives. Self-esteem is needed to live and experience life joyfully. Once you achieve self-esteem, then it reflects in the way you handle life and its myriad challenges. Self-esteem can be defined in many ways including:
- A sense of self-worth and self-belief in one's own capabilities
- How good or bad you feel about yourself and your worth
- Your overall evaluation of your emotional, physical, and mental well-being

Signs of Low Self-Esteem

Look out for these signs that subtly or obviously reflect your low self-esteem:

Self Esteem For Women

You keep apologizing unnecessarily – This sign can be easily missed and misinterpreted for politeness. However, look again closely at instances when you have said sorry needlessly. For example, if you bump into someone accidentally, do you instinctively apologize without even seeing whose fault it was? If this is the case, you could be a victim of low self-esteem. Your apology could be rooted in a misconceived belief that everything that is going wrong is your fault.

You attribute everything to luck – If you get a promotion in your office, do you say, "I was lucky," or "I feel blessed?" If yes, this could mean that you don't know how to give credit to yourself for good results; a typical symptom of low self-esteem. You believe that something good happened to you not because you are worthy of it but because of divine intervention or luck. The belief in the divine is not an issue. Your lack of belief in your worth is the disturbing thought. You don't like to accept compliments and praise because of this lack of self-belief.

You do things that you don't really like – For example, you could be buying dresses that you are not really comfortable in or refurbishing your home in a way that is not your taste just to appear fashionable and trendy. Ask yourself how many times you have invited that girl whom you hate to all your parties. Ponder these choices and questions, and see if they are driven by a need to please others; this is another key element that reflects low self-esteem.

You are afraid of conflicts and making mistakes – If you hate having conflicts with anyone in your life, then it could be a sign of low self-esteem because you don't want to say anything that is confrontational. You hate to make mistakes because you are afraid of failures.

Other common signs of low self-esteem include sensitivity to criticism, social withdrawal, hostility (typically to hide the feeling of low self-esteem), and being excessively preoccupied with personal problems. Low self-esteem also is reflected through physical symptoms such as frequent headaches, fatigue, and insomnia.

Signs of High Self-Esteem

Here are some signs of high self-esteem:
- You are not afraid of making mistakes.
- You have no problems accepting compliments proudly but without arrogance.
- You are not overly sensitive to criticism.
- You are willing to take risks.
- You don't let others disrespect you or abuse you and your abilities.

Why Do Women have Low Self-Esteem?

The foundations for our self-esteem are laid at very early developmental stages. Much before our brains develop complex cognitive systems, we are exposed to feelings of shame, guilt, and pride through the interactions we have with our primary caregivers. These early-stage basic foundations influence the

Self Esteem For Women

way we think of ourselves in our adulthood.

Additionally, girls seem to be at a disadvantage when it comes to self-esteem because our society 'expects' girls to behave 'nicely' whereas boys 'can be boys,' where misbehavior is seen as an unavoidable natural instinct. Therefore, girls experience failure and rejection with a lot more intensity than boys. Women think about their feelings of shame and guilt for a sustained period of time, enhancing their feelings of low self-esteem.

High expectations (such as those listed below) result in low self-esteem in women:
- Little girls are supposed to stay away from tussles and fights; those are reserved for the boys.
- Little girls are expected to avoid aggressive behaviors of all kinds to the extent that if they choose aggressive sports, then women are treated disdainfully.
- They are expected to behave nicely so that they are ready for matrimony; many times, this is at the cost of their dreams and desires.
- Women are expected to be 'perfect' in all ways. Many women reject those parts of themselves which are not aligned with societal expectations, meeting this bizarre and extremely unreasonable demand for perfection, resulting in low self-esteem.
- In the modern world, perfection includes having a 'perfect' body' too. Social media and print media are replete with movie stars, and their 'perfectly' toned bodies and unblemished faces drive the desire of the average women to reach those unreasonable levels. Marketers take advantage of these desires and sell

unrealistic dreams to women. Self-esteem takes a big beating when women fail to achieve these dreams.
- And, if some women do manage to break these stereotypes and do well for themselves, they are expected to downplay their achievements and be modest, and not 'show off.'
- Women who talk proudly about their qualifications are called braggarts, whereas men talking about the same qualifications are called 'confident achievers.'

All these negativity-focused reasons drive uncertainty in women, and most of them are scared of or even unaware of their inherent abilities. Their self-talk focuses only on their weaknesses and inabilities, with little or no thought to their real powers and strengths. The final result is very low self-esteem.

Importance of Self-Esteem

High self-esteem uplifts you whereas low self-esteem drags you down. With high self-esteem, you will be able to achieve your highest potential and live life to please yourself. Of course, people with high self-esteem understand that pleasing oneself does not mean hurting others. It only means you are in the driver's seat of your life.

With high self-esteem comes high levels of confidence and assertiveness. Your belief in your capabilities and your acceptance of your weaknesses help you to be confident and assert yourself without feeling arrogant or victimized.

Self Esteem For Women

Self-Discovery Questions on Your Current Level of Self-Esteem

Answer the following questions honestly, and you will get a fairly good idea of your current level of self-esteem. You can begin your journey to build your self-esteem from this place.

- Do you think you are a boring person?
- Do you think you are always messing up things?
- Do you believe your absence will be felt at a party or any social gathering?
- Do you think your loved ones don't trust your capabilities?
- Do you believe you are not worthy of anything?
- Do you take yourself to be a complete failure?
- Do you believe you can match the capabilities of other people in any given social setup?
- Do you think you can achieve your highest potential?
- Do you think you deserve to be loved?

Self Esteem For Women

Chapter 2: The Components of Building Self-Esteem

"Self-esteem is a powerful force within each of us ... Self-esteem is the experience that we are appropriate to life and to the requirements of life," said Nathaniel Branden. He was a close associate of the highly celebrated author Ayn Rand and an eminent psychotherapist in his own right. Branden spoke at length about self-esteem and its six important components in his famous book, The Six Pillars of Self-Esteem.

The six pillars of self-esteem, according to Nathaniel Branden, include:
1. The Practice of Living Consciously
2. The Practice of Self-Acceptance
3. The Practice of Self-Responsibility
4. The Practice of Self-Assertiveness
5. The Practice of Living Purposefully
6. The Practice of Personal Integrity
7. Let's look at each of them in a little bit of detail.

The Practice of Living Consciously

How many times have you felt that you are drifting through life without knowing how you reached where you are now or where you are going next? You live each day like an automaton; eating, sleeping, doing the routine things and everything else without being conscious of your feelings and thoughts. This is the state of most women of the modern day as they struggle to juggle their careers, homes, and many other social expectations.

Lao Tzu said, *"If you are depressed, you are living in the past. If you are anxious, you are living in the future. If you are at peace, you are living in the present."* Living consciously helps you live in the moment, helping you experience life more meaningfully than before.

A key element in living consciously is being acutely aware of your thoughts and emotions.

Take the example of cooking the evening meal for your family.

Today, focus on your thoughts and emotions while your body is engaged in the cooking activity.

Are your thoughts about the cooking, the smells, the ingredients that are going into the dish, the measurement of these ingredients, the texture of the dish, etc.? Or are your thoughts on something that happened in the office during the day or an impending argument you are planning with your partner when he returns? Or are the thoughts simply random and you have no idea what you are thinking? Now, focus on the emotions while you are cooking. Are you happy? Sad? Angry? Just okay, with no particular feelings?

Cooking consciously requires you to focus your thoughts, emotions, and your entire being on that one activity. Your self-awareness increases when you indulge consciously in each of your tasks. When you are aware of every element that is occupying your body, mind, and spirit, you begin to see things that were hitherto invisible because you did not focus on them. With this newly widened perspective, you can manage difficult situations in a much better way than before.

Living consciously is the most important step to increase self-awareness, and with increased self-awareness comes self-improvement and improved self-esteem.

The Practice of Self-Acceptance

"Wanting to be someone else is a waste of the person you are," advised Marilyn Monroe, and acceptance of this one truth can positively impact the life of every woman on this planet. You are unique, beautiful, and complete in yourself. Chasing after things that take away this uniqueness is an unworthy and useless activity.

We saw how, when you live consciously, your level of self-awareness increases considerably. Being self-aware means you know your strengths, your capabilities, and your weaknesses. Self-acceptance simply means being fine with how you are right now.

So, you cook wonderfully, and your family loves every dish you turn out. Self-acceptance means accepting this trait proudly, but not with arrogance, which is not a difficult thing to do. Now, take, for example, a lack of great fashion sense. Accepting this weakness without a feeling of guilt and being okay with it is what self-acceptance is about.

Self-acceptance does not mean you will not work to overcome your weaknesses. In fact, self-acceptance does not mean liking or disliking a trait. It only means you are fine with how you are for the moment. Self-acceptance enhances self-love, and when you love yourself, you do not need anyone else to love you and make you complete. This sense of being complete is a significant contributor to your self-esteem.

Like Ayn Rand said, *"To say 'I love you,' one must be ready to say the 'I'!"* When you accept yourself the way you are, you will happily accept others the way they are, which will help you lead a far more harmonious life than before.

The Practice of Self-Responsibility

Self-responsibility is a sign of strength. Only powerful and strong people take responsibility for themselves and their lives. Mediocrity encourages blaming others, whereas excellence urges you to take control of your life.

Dr. Wayne Dyer, one of the influential thinkers of the modern times, said, *"Everything you do is based on the choices you make. It's not your parents, your past relationships, your job, the economy, the weather, an argument, or your age that is to blame. You and only you are responsible for every decision and choice you make."*

You have learned to live consciously. You have learned the art of self-acceptance. The next step to improved self-esteem is to take responsibility for your life and sit in the driver's seat. Your happiness is in your hands. If you are sad, then you choose to be sad, as it is possible to find positivity even in the bleakest of situations.

Susan B. Anthony has a constitutional amendment named after her. She was one of the pioneers who fought for women's rights to vote in the US. She took responsibility for the wrongs happening in her life. She strongly believed in her right to vote and did not wait for men to come forward and fight for her. Although Susan B. Anthony did not live to see the beneficial outcome of her fight, her name is cast in stone in American history because the 19th Amendment, giving US women suffrage rights, is called the Susan B. Anthony Amendment.

It is important that you learn lessons from such powerful women and take responsibility for your life. For example, if you have a problem with your fashion sense, then take lessons from someone you trust. If there is no such person in your life, there are many grooming classes available where you can pick up this skill. The critical thing to self-responsibility is to stop blaming others for your problems, and instead, find ways to overcome them.

The Practice of Self-Assertiveness

Assertiveness is a critical personality trait that helps you win arguments and get some extra brownie points at a negotiation table. Assertiveness is an external trait that reflects the strength of your powers as well as the humility you have when it comes to accepting your weaknesses.

Self-assertiveness includes all the above plus a little more. Self-assertiveness calls for being true to yourself. It calls for reflecting your inner personality to the outside world. Self-assertiveness is the exact opposite of presenting a façade to the other people around you while you have a completely different personality within. It is the trait of authenticity. Self-assertiveness calls for living your dreams and desires the way you want to, and not to please someone else.

Dr. Elizabeth Blackwell was the first woman who graduated with a medical degree from an American medical college. If she had not the self-assertiveness qualities, the modern world, perhaps, would have to wait a little longer before women were allowed into medical schools to earn degrees and practice medicine.

"The most fundamental aggression to ourselves, the most fundamental harm we can do to ourselves, is to remain ignorant by not having the courage and the respect to look at ourselves honestly and gently," says Pema Chodron, the celebrated American Tibetan Buddhist, and an ordained Buddhist nun.

Live consciously, accept yourself, take self-responsibility, and be self-assertive to build self-esteem slowly but steadily in a way that it will never leave your side. Self-assertiveness requires you to speak your mind even in the face of adversity and unpopularity.

For example, if you believe in disciplining your children from a young age, then there will be times when you will have to make unpopular calls that could make your children dislike or even hate you for a while. It is indeed a difficult thing for a mother to accept this situation. But, if your self-assertiveness is at a healthy level, then you will find the courage to handle this temporary unpleasantness and discipline. Your kids will thank you for it, later on. But, right now, you will need to be self-assertive to do what is best for your kids.

The Practice of Living with a Purpose

John F. Kennedy said, *"Efforts and courage are wasted without direction and purpose."* Look back at your life and think of the most glorious moments. Recall why the moments were so glorious that those feelings are deeply etched in your psyche. One of the prominent reasons that will stand out is that they were a moment of achieving a predetermined purpose.

Whether it was graduating college with flying colors, getting that coveted promotion, or helping your mother through a difficult illness, having a purpose enhances the joy of outcome. A purposeless life is like a rudderless ship that drifts along where the elements of nature choose to take it.

Your life undergoes a paradigm shift when you know the

purpose that guides and drives you. The Triune Brain Model, proposed by Paul MacLean, the famed 1960s neuroscientist, says that the human brain consists of three parts including the reptilian or the instinctual part, the mammalian or the emotional part, and the primate or the thinking part.

The reptilian part of the brain handles things like territory and aggression. The mammalian part manages the food and sex. The primate or the thinking part handles deeper elements like complex concepts, perception, planning, etc. This primate part of the brain knows that you need meaning and purpose in your life for fulfillment.

Elizabeth Gilbert, the author of the international bestseller, *Eat, Pray, Love,*' discovered her purpose for writing while she was traveling to heal from a painful divorce. She traveled to Italy, India, and Bali in search of enjoyment, devotion, and balance. These travels helped her discover her purpose which, in turn, brought her success and happiness. Before that, she was living an average life, thinking she was happy in her marriage.

It is only when you put your mind to the concept of living purposefully that you can live life meaningfully and sublimely experience each moment. Life with a purpose will ensure you are not drifting along thoughtlessly merely going where circumstances choose to take you. You don't need to travel the world to find your life's purpose. Sit down with a pen and paper, and find answers to the self-assessment questions given at the end of this chapter to discover your real purpose in life.

A life purpose should be based on your dreams and desires, and not be passed on from influencers in your life like your parents, spouse, teachers, bosses, etc. Once you have clearly defined the primary purpose of your life, then you must endeavor to break it up into measurable, time-bound goals so that you can keep track of your progress and make suitable changes if needed.

The Practice of Personal Integrity

You can see how you have progressed in building your self-esteem. You started with learning to live consciously, then accepting yourself the way you are, warts and all; learned to take self-responsibility for your life and the choices you make; learned the importance of self-assertiveness; and then began living with a deep sense of purpose.

As you progress through each of the five pillars, you will find the strength of self-esteem building even as you enhance your self-awareness and become comfortable living life with yourself and on your terms. The sixth and the last pillar, namely "The Practice of Personal Integrity," gives an enormous amount of strength to your self-esteem.

Personal Integrity is living a life based on the values and principles you have chosen to be your guiding light. The more you lead a life that is aligned with those chosen personal values, the higher your self-esteem will grow. Living a life aligned with your values enhances your self-belief to lead a fulfilling and meaningful life, overcoming challenges on your own which, in turn, directly impacts self-esteem levels positively.

Self Esteem For Women

If Mother Teresa had not had the deep sense of personal integrity needed to stand up for what she truly believed in, she could not have become the beacon of light for the most underprivileged people in India. Although a part of her life was dedicated to underprivileged Indians, her work in other parts of the world did not go unnoticed, which is why she was conferred the Nobel Peace Prize in 1979!

To practice personal integrity, you have to earn the 'unpopular' tag quite often. For example, if you have an office project to finish by the end of the day, you might have to say no to a get-together lunch with your colleagues because that will delay your work in the evening. Although these negative responses might be aligned with your personal integrity, they could make you unpopular with your colleagues, and it is possible that you might not get many invitations in the future.

The practice of personal integrity is a tough road to take as it can turn very lonely. However, this final pillar considerably enhances the power of your self-esteem.

Self-esteem is not about achieving perfection. It is the simple acceptance of yourself, including strengths and weaknesses. Self-esteem is accepting a particular situation and knowing that you are not equipped to handle it, and either choosing to seek help (if possible) or making choices that are aligned with your abilities. Self-esteem does not come from being confident in your current state of skills. It comes from your ability to learn and build new skills for self-improvement. To be in a constant state of learning, you have to move out of your comfort zone. The more you learn, the more confidence you will build which,

Self Esteem For Women

in turn, will help in developing your self-esteem.

Self-Assssment Section
Answer the questions under each of the six components of self-esteem. This exercise will help you gauge your current status on all of them. You can use the self-knowledge gained from these self-assessment exercises to create an effective and efficient plan to develop your self-esteem.

Self-Questions to Gauge Your Present State of Conscious Life
1. Did you choose your career consciously, or did you take it simply because it came your way?
2. Do you do jobs that are given to you, or do you pick up jobs that you love to do?
3. Are you doing activities simply to fill up your waking hours, or are you doing activities that give you joy and happiness?
4. Are you conscious of the progress of time, or do you just drift through the day, uncertain of how you spend your waking hours?
5. Do you focus on each activity to identify and appreciate how it is contributing to your growth, or do you unconsciously do each task thoughtlessly?
6. Are you aware of how your money is being spent, or do you simply live from one paycheck to the next?

Self-Questions to Gauge Your Present State of Self-Acceptance
1. Are you living life to meet your desires or someone else's?

2. Do you forgive yourself easily?
3. Do you love yourself enough to know you should begin to look after yourself?
4. Do you accept yourself enough to know that you need good food, exercise, and sufficient rest to lead a fulfilling life?
5. Do you accept your past mistakes by letting them go out of your life?
6. Do you accept yourself so that you can commit to things you know you can achieve and say no to things you know you cannot achieve?
7. Do you give yourself sufficient me-time during which you indulge in activities with yourself?
8. Are you comfortable when you are alone?

Self-Questions to Gauge Your Present State of Self-Responsibility

1. Do you believe you give your best in everything you do? If no, write down the reasons.
2. Do you believe you set reasonably high standards for yourself so that you can improve yourself? If no, why not?
3. Do you start any work with the feeling, "Oh! This is impossible to do?" If yes, ask yourself why?
4. Do you believe you take sufficient time and effort to do all your tasks in the best possible way? If no, why not?
5. Do you believe you are doing enough to prevent distractions, procrastination, and temptations from getting the better of you? If no, why not?
6. Do you believe you optimally use all the resources available to you? If no, what is stopping you?
7. Do you believe you seek help when you need it? If no,

why not?
8. Do you believe you review your work to ensure errors are minimized? If no, why not?
9. Do you believe you do research and find the best solutions for the various problems in your life? If no, why not?

Self-Questions to Gauge Your Present State of Self-Assertiveness
1. Do you think you say yes often, even when you want to say no?
2. Do you think you hide your thoughts and emotions if the person you are speaking to is a stranger?
3. Are you afraid to give negative feedback because you don't like to be unpopular?
4. Do you believe it is easier to pretend to say something nice even if it is not true?
5. Do you think that in your efforts to keep everyone happy, you are contradicting yourself?
6. Do you think you are comfortable in a face-to-face interaction?

Self-Questions to Gauge Your Present State of Living Purposefully
1. Do you think your purpose in life is your own, or borrowed from your parents?
2. Can you clearly talk about the journey of your life until now, and where you are headed in the future?
3. Is your perception about yourself based on others' perceptions about yourself? For example, do you believe

you are a 'bad' cook because your mother thought so? Or that you are 'bad' at math because your teacher in your school thought so?
4. Do you think you are walking a life path that you truly believe in?
5. Do you know your life's purpose?
6. Where do you see yourself five or ten years from now? Have you written down your goals?
7. Do you keep track of the progress you have made?

Self-Questions to Gauge Your Present State of Personal Integrity

1. Do you believe that, in today's society, we have to cheat or lie to succeed?
2. Do you think that people who take ethical shortcuts succeed more than those who choose not to?
3. Are you happy with your level of ethics and personal integrity?
4. Do you think you can lie about your home address if it is the only way to get your child admitted to a good school?
5. Do you think you are doing enough to build personal integrity in your children?
6. Do you often lie to your friends and family?
7. Do you often lie to your bosses and colleagues?
8. Do you show exaggerated expense claims for any overseas office trips?

Chapter 3: Habits and How to Use Them for the Good

Charles Duhigg is a bestselling author and Pulitzer Prize winner, and one of his most famous work is titled, *The Power of Habit."* In this book, Charles Duhigg talks at length about the habit loop and how it is possible to fit any habit into this loop which includes three elements, namely:
1. The Cue
2. The Routine
3. The Reward

This chapter is dedicated to giving you some insights into these three elements of the habit loop, and how you can use them to get rid of old bad habits and replace them with new good ones. Let's look at each of these three elements of the habit loop.

The Cue

The cue is the trigger that puts your brain into automatic mode and brings in the specific routine. The cue initiates the habitual behavior or routine. The trigger for setting in the habit can be a person, a location, emotion, or anything else. It is challenging to identify the cue(s) that trigger the routine of any particular habit. Changing a bad habit requires you to first identify the cue(s).

Fortunately, psychologists have categorized all cues into five basic types including time, location, a preceding event, emotional state, and other people. Let us look at each of the five types in a bit of detail to help you identify what is triggering your bad habit.

The time cue – This is the most common cue for any habit. Look at your daily schedule, and you will understand why time is the most common cue for habits. You wake up at a particular time, have your meals at specific times, go to bed at a certain time, etc. Now let us look at an example of a bad habit that depends on the time cue.

Suppose you go for your morning coffee break at 11 a.m. each day. You join your colleagues in the office cafeteria. Your coffee always includes a doughnut or a cookie, which is causing weight gain. You want to stop this habit of eating a cookie or doughnut during this break. When you recognize the cue, you can make changes so that you respond differently to that cue.

So, your cue is the 11 a.m. break. Instead of going to the cafeteria, you can choose to drink your coffee at your desk so that you are not tempted to have the doughnut or cookie. Or, you can carry a box of freshly-cut fruits which you can have during the break.

The location cue – This is another powerful habit creator. You automatically turn on the light when you enter a particular room. You automatically shut the bathroom door once you are inside. All these actions or routines are habitual, and your brain kicks the routine in as soon as it recognizes the location cue.

How many times have you walked into your kitchen to unwittingly reach out for the cookie jar or chips container? That is the power of the location cue. It is so deeply ingrained in your psyche that your brain automatically drives your sense organs to perform the routine; in this case, reaching out for the cookie jar. Here is a classic way of using the power of the habit to do something healthy. Instead of cookies, place some fruit in the jar. So, when you reach your hand into the jar, you get healthy fruit instead of cookies. Alternately, put the cookie jar somewhere that is not easily accessible.

Therefore, identifying the cue has given you solutions that facilitate the change of habit or eliminating the habit.

The preceding event cue – When your phone rings, don't you automatically pick it up? After you finish your call, don't you invariably look for an email or social media notifications? That is a classic example of a preceding event cue.

You can use this cue to build great habits. For example, you can choose to wait for your phone to ring at least four times before picking it up. Focus on your breath while you wait to pick up your phone. This approach will prepare you for managing the call more effectively, irrespective of who the call is from. Every time your phone rings, create a habit of focusing on your breath. You may not be able to concentrate on more than one or two inhalations and exhalations. However, even this small habit can be of immense help because your brain is now being attuned to something positive. In fact, this approach slows you down, which is a good thing in this modern, rushing, hither-thither world.

Another great example of a preceding event cue: While you wait for your morning coffee to brew, invariably you are checking your phone again or letting your thoughts go randomly all over the place. Use these couple of minutes to meditate. Focus on your thoughts and emotions and be mindful of them. This morning meditation sets the perfect tone for the entire day.

One more example that all of us can easily relate to is eating while watching TV. Before you switched on the TV, you were not hungry and did not want to eat anything. As soon as you sit on the couch and turn on the power button on the TV remote, your brain goes into eating mode. Without even pausing to think, you have walked into the kitchen and brought out a bag of chips to munch on while watching TV.

Identify and recognize this common precedent event cue, and find ways not to indulge in eating while watching TV. One option is not to watch TV until your brain is rewired not to relate TV watching with binge-eating. Another option is to ensure you have no junk food lying around at home. Instead, stock your fridge with fruits and vegetables to make yourself a healthy salad to munch on while you watch TV.

The emotional state cue – Your emotional state is more often a trigger for a bad habit than a good one. For example, when you are depressed, do you binge-eat? When you are angry, do you scream and shout? When you are upset, do you shop for unnecessary things? All these are classic examples of emotional state cues.

The problematic thing about emotion-based cues is that they are very tough to control because, during a heightened emotional state, your feelings are bound to overwhelm and rule you. It takes a lot of effort to manage emotions to prevent them from overwhelming you.

Therefore, in the initial stages of identifying bad habits based on this kind of cue, it is best to avoid trying to replace them with a good habit. An excellent way to manage these conditions is to practice mindfulness. As your feelings engulf you, step outside of them, and watch the emotions as objectively as you can. Let yourself think, "Yes, I am angry because …" However, try and not respond to the feelings. Just watch them as a witness.

Initially, this method is going to be tough because you are habituated to reacting to your emotions. However, with patient and persistent practice, you will see that this method of observing your emotion without reacting to them becomes increasingly easy.

Soon, you will notice that emotions are one of the most transient aspects of human nature. A situation that triggered anger in you yesterday may make you laugh out loud today. Mindfulness helps you recognize these emotional states, and when you focus on the feelings, the brain is prevented from going into automatic mode.

The 'other people' cue – Jim Rohn, a highly influential American author, entrepreneur, and motivational speaker, says, *"You are the average of the five people you spend the most time with."* It is very easy to verify this observation in your life.

Have you noticed how much you eat when you have your meal with people who overeat? If you had been mindful, would you have seen that you eat far more than your usual amount? Similarly, if you are having a meal with people who eat consciously, you will also unwittingly follow their habits. This is how 'other people' affect the way you form your habits.

For example, if you don't usually drink, but are in the company of friends who drink, it is natural to get yourself a drink. This attitude is only a response to the environment and the behavior of the people around you. If you can identify such 'other people' in your life who influence bad habits, it makes sense to stay away from them as much as possible.

The Routine

The routine is the actual habit, which could be emotional, physical, or mental. The routine part of the loop is easily recognizable. For example, eating that cookie during your morning break or when you visit the kitchen is the routine.

The Reward

The reward is the end result that appears worthwhile for your brain to set up the habit formation or the remembering and recalling routine for future use. The 'reward' is a misnomer in a bad habit. In truth, there is no reward because bad habits result in emotional, financial, and physical losses. However, the brain (driven by the 'sense of temporary satisfaction' given by the habit) believes the 'reward' is worthwhile and creates the habit loop so that the automatic mode is set in once the cue comes into play.

Therefore, to break bad habits, you must try and experiment with different rewards that are truly worthwhile so that your brain creates the loop for good habits. For example, runners get a 'high' while running and gamblers get the same 'high' while gambling. So, if you can replace running with gambling, your brain will believe it is worthwhile to run and will create the remembering and recalling loop for the good habit.

The Importance of Identifying the Habit Loop

Identifying the habit loop in each of your habits can help you manage your habits more positively than before in two ways:
- Cues can help in creating new good habits
- Cues can help in breaking and/or replacing bad habits

Changing habits is tough. However, identifying the habit loop simplifies the process of giving up bad habits and creating new ones. Identifying the structure of a habit helps you find solutions to make positive changes in your life. Essentially, identifying your habit loops enhances your self-awareness which, in turn, enables you to find innovative solutions to overcome bad habits.

Replacing Old Bad Habits with New Good Ones

"Depending on what they are, our habits will either make us or break us. We become what we repeatedly do." —Sean Covey. Therefore, it makes sense to eliminate bad habits and create good habits.

Eliminating old bad habits is really not possible because the worth of the reward associated with the habit is deeply etched in our brains. For example, flopping on the couch after returning from work can never really be eradicated from your mind because neurological patterns are already in place.

However, if you can construct new neurological patterns that deliver the same level of satisfaction as flopping on the couch, then these old patterns will get replaced with the new ones. For example, if you quickly begin your walk or run after returning from work, then your brain will slowly but surely replace this neurological pattern over the old one, helping you overcome the bad habit and create a new good one.

The trick is to keep the same cue and reward (because these two cannot really be changed) and experiment with new and worthier routines than the earlier ones to replace bad habits with good ones. So, in the above example, the cue is a combination of time and location—the location is the couch after returning from work, and the reward is the satisfaction received from the happy chemicals. The routine is flopping on the couch. Now, keep the cue and reward constant, and instead of flopping on the couch, go for a run or visit the gym. Effectively, you have broken the bad habit and replaced it with a good habit.

Self-Assessment Questions On Your Current Level of Habits
Answer the following questions which will help you understand your current level of habits:
1. Do you believe you are a dependable worker?
2. Do you think you are a dependable mother, relentlessly doing all the regular activities needed for your children?
3. Do you believe you are a punctual person?
4. Are you a great collaborator, ensuring team meetings are held productively?
5. Do you think you are a disciplined and responsible worker who does not need to be supervised?
6. Can you recognize the top five bad habits you are keen on getting rid of?

Self Esteem For Women

Chapter 4: Practical Examples

We discussed the six components of self-esteem in Chapter 2 and how it is important to build each one of them to take your self-esteem up a few notches. This chapter is dedicated to giving you some tips, based on practical examples, to develop the six components.

The Practice of Living Consciously

NLP Techniques
Neuro-Linguistic Programming or NLP is designed to align your subconscious and unconscious minds with your conscious mind so that your entire being is moving harmoniously in the same direction. NLP stands for:
- Neuro – relates to the brain's nerves and the neuro-systems
- Linguistic – relates to the language of the mind

- Programming – makes something work in a particular way

Here are a couple of popular NLP techniques to help you live more consciously than before.

Focus on your thoughts – Our subconscious and unconscious minds are deeply affected by our thoughts. For example, if you think that you are not going to get that promotion, then your conscious mind and your physical body will resist your attempts to prepare for the promotion because your negative thoughts are forcing your deeper mind to believe the thought to be true.

However, if your thoughts are, "I deserve that promotion, and I will definitely get it," then your subconscious mind will believe this to be true and will drive your conscious mind and your physical body to work hard and achieve your promotion.

Prayers – Prayers represent your wishes and hopes. Prayers render a deep sense of faith that there is a higher power that is working with you to help you realize your dreams.

For example, if you pray for your son to do well on his SAT exams, then your subconscious mind feels empowered to encourage your son to work hard and believe in his capabilities to achieve success. Your faith in your son's capabilities and strengths will pass on to him, urging him to give his best, considerably enhancing his chances for success.

Self Esteem For Women

Affirmations
Affirmations empower you to believe in yourself and your abilities to achieve success. Use the following positive affirmations to live more consciously than before:
- I am my own master and need no one else to be complete
- I use my energies constructively and productively
- I feel happy when I make conscious choices and live life on my terms
- I am acutely tuned in to my thoughts and emotions.

Visualization
Davin Alexander is a famous author of many bestselling cookbooks and a TV reality show hostess. She is a firm believer in creating vision boards to help her achieve her dreams. She says creating your dreams into a visual in your mind is a powerful reminder of your future dreams and goals.

Visualization is nothing but a vision board in your mind. All of us have a powerful imagination and it makes sense to use it effectively to live consciously. Visualize victories and happy days. Work towards crystallizing those mind visuals.

Meditation
Meditation is about spending time with your thoughts and emotions. When you meditate, you are focusing on your feelings and thoughts, many times even unpleasant ones too. When you connect with these emotions and thoughts, you get to know them better and discern between the useful and wasteful ones so you can discard the bad ones and put good thoughts to effective use.

Start and end your day with a ten-minute meditation. During this meditation, visualize how your day will unfold, and prepare yourself for the expected good and bad events. You can also use positive affirmations during your meditation session.

Maintaining a Diary
Maintaining a diary facilitates improved conscious living in multiple ways:

First, it enhances the experiences of the day as you relive them while making entries in your diary. For example, if your boss paid you a compliment, it is possible that you were so busy that you did not have time to revel in the joy. When you make this entry in your diary at the end of the day, you can recall this event and experience the happiness of the moment in a more wholesome manner than earlier.

You can feel the happiness for having worked hard and gotten praise from your boss. Now, if you remember that someone else in your team should also get a piece of this goodwill, then this might be the best time to pass on the compliments to that person too. It is natural to have forgotten to mention this team member's name to your boss when he said those nice things earlier in the day.

Second, maintaining a diary enhances your sense of gratitude as well. Being grateful for small things helps you live more consciously than before. And finally, you can look at the negative experiences of the day with detachment, learn from them, and move on.

The Practice of Self-Acceptance

NLP Techniques
Anchoring for self-acceptance – Whenever you feel overwhelmed by some weakness, you need to reassure yourself that your strengths are sufficiently good to make up for this weakness. Anchoring is an amazing NLP technique that helps you recall happy moments by connecting them to a physical gesture.

For example, recall a happy memory, and as you relive the experience, rub the tips of your thumb and forefinger together. Every time you think of this memory, perform this gesture so that the experience is 'anchored' in your brain. Whenever you doubt yourself, repeat this action, and the positive image will fill your head, and you will regain control of your positivity.

Affirmations
Self-acceptance is an important element of self-esteem. Use any of the following affirmations for self-acceptance:
- I am worthy of happiness, joy, and love
- I will be loved only when I love myself
- I am unique, and that is the best thing about me
- I love myself unconditionally, and therefore, I can love others the same way
- I completely approve of myself
- I do not need anything or anyone other than myself to make me complete
- I will use the gift of life with confidence and exuberance

- I will surround myself with positivity because I deserve only that

Visualization
Always visualize yourself in a smiling and happy mood. Always focus on the good things in your life and visualize them. Automatically, you will get a smile on your face, and a smiling face will never fail to attract positivity and happy people and situations.

For example, when you think of something nice and pleasant, a smile comes up on your face without even you realizing it. Similarly, when you think of a terrible incident in your life, then either your face gets a frown or tears well up. Similarly, when you love and accept yourself the way you are, your confidence will reflect in your body language, taking your self-esteem a few notches up.

Meditation
Use the self-acceptance affirmations given above and meditate on them regularly so that your conscious, subconscious, and unconscious minds are all aligned with each other, helping you live a more harmonious and happy life than before.

Maintaining a Diary
Use the following prompts to make entries in your diary:
- What are the things that I have in my life that I know I deserve completely?
- How can I trust myself more?

- Was there an incident in your life that you believed was not right when it took place? However, now you know it was for the best. Write down the details of that incident.

The Practice of Self-Responsibility

NLP Techniques

The Swish technique – The Swish technique is used to convert negative thoughts into positive ones. Let us take a typical scenario in your life to explain it. Suppose you are having a dinner party. You are an excellent cook, and yet, your mind is full of doubts about whether all the dishes will turn out well. The Swish technique has three components, including:

The unwanted thought or trigger – This is the negative, self-doubting thoughts about your cooking skills.

The unwanted feeling – This is the feeling of fear and insecurity that comes with the negative trigger.

The replacement thought – Now, think of a time when you received great praise for your cooking skills. Replace the negative trigger with happy thoughts associated with the earlier success. Keep replacing the unwanted triggers with replacement thoughts until your mind is rewired to think positively.

The Swish NLP technique works excellently to eliminate baseless doubts in your mind so that you can take responsibility

Self Esteem For Women

for yourself to work hard and achieve great outcomes.

Affirmations
Here are some powerful affirmations for personal responsibility:
- I take full responsibility for all the choices and experiences in my life.
- Only I am responsible for my life.
- I am not responsible for others' perception of me.
- I am entirely accountable for my actions, feelings, words, and thoughts, irrespective of what triggered them.

Visualization
Visualization of a future event or of a future time in your life helps you build self-responsibility to work towards achieving it. Here is an example of how to use visualization:
- First, find a calm place and sit comfortably.
- Next, close your eyes, and imagine how you see yourself five years from today.
- What do you see? A promotion? A happy home, filled with the joyous laughter of your loving children? Traveling the world? Pick one that is the most important for you.
- At this stage, don't doubt that you will achieve what you see in your mind. Simply fill in all the details in the image, and feel the visual coming to life. Etch this image in your mind.
- Open your eyes, and feel the joy of the visualization experience.
- Take responsibility for this dream, and begin your work to achieve it.

Self Esteem For Women

Meditation

Whenever something goes wrong in your life, your mind gets filled with negative thoughts, and by default, you choose to find someone else to blame. Don't be ashamed of this reaction. This is natural. However, when you live consciously, you will be acutely aware of this feeling.

Now, sit down comfortably, and relive the negative experience with your eyes closed. Remember to keep out the emotions during the meditation. Let us take an example. Suppose you were asked to do a presentation by your boss, and you did what you believed was right.

Now, the presentation does not go as well as it should have. Your boss gets angry and says something nasty to you in front of your colleagues. You could blame your boss for not checking your work earlier. However, that is not a healthy sign of taking self-responsibility.

Instead of reacting with anger, ask for permission and leave the meeting for a few minutes. Go to a calm place and reflect on the experience. Ask yourself the following questions:
- Why did you not ask for clarification and confirm whether your line of thought aligned with your boss' expectations?
- Why did you not ask your boss to look at your work and request feedback so that you could have made the corrections ahead of time?

Focus on the entire experience, and take self-responsibility for those elements that you could have done right, without waiting for anyone else. This approach will let you take control of your life and do the right things in the future. Mistakes are not to be taken personally, even if they come with some humiliation. Take mistakes in the right spirit, learn from them, and let them go.

Maintaining a Diary

At the end of each day, write two things that went wrong during the day. Recall the experiences and relive them in your mind, minus the emotions. Now, beside each of these experiences, write at least two ways you could have done something different so that the outcomes would not have been as bad as they turned out. Repeat this exercise every day, and you will notice how the power of self-responsibility improves the quality of your life.

The Practice of Self-Assertiveness

NLP Techniques

Learning to say no is one of the most critical lessons taught in NLP. Self-assertiveness calls for you to say no quite often in your life. How many times have you babysat for your neighbor while she partied with her friends simply because you couldn't find the courage to say no? How many times have you accepted more work than you can manage because you do not know how to say no or are scared you will lose your favorite spot in your boss' mind?

All these are classic examples of failing to practice self-assertiveness. You know saying no is the right thing to do, and it is aligned with your values and principles. And yet, fearing the unpopularity tag, you choose to be bullied into taking on more than your capability. Instead of losing out on self-assertiveness, build the necessary skills to become more assertive.

One of the most popular NLP techniques to learn how to say no is deconstructing and formulating desired scenarios. Practice responses and reactions in your mind, and use them in real-life scenarios. For example, if you have to say no to your neighbor the next time she asks for you to babysit her child while she goes partying, think of appropriate responses as to how you will deal with her in your mind. Formulate compelling answers to her expected counter-questions and practice them in your mind. The more you practice, the easier it will be to use them in real-life scenarios.

Affirmations
Repeat these affirmations to develop a natural sense of self-assertiveness so that you can express your emotions and thoughts honestly. These affirmations help in building your mental strength to increase your self-assertiveness.
- I am not afraid to speak my mind.
- I am an assertive person.
- I readily let others know my feelings.
- I am very confident when speaking to others.
- I stand firm and resolute when my core values are challenged.
- I stand up for my principles.
- I am confident of controlling my responses and reactions in any situation.
- I express myself honestly and strongly.

Self Esteem For Women

- I set clear standards and boundaries.
- I am respected for my self-assertiveness.

Visualization

Let us take an example of a situation wherein you have to give a presentation to your senior bosses. You are a great worker and that is why you have been chosen for this task. And yet, your lack of self-assertiveness skills puts you into a panic mode. Here is where visualization techniques will be of immense help.

First, make sure you are thoroughly prepared with your presentation. Practice repeatedly so that the presentation is deeply ingrained in your mind and you know it by rote, without any mistakes. Next, sit comfortably and close your eyes.

Visualize the room where all your seniors are sitting, waiting for you to start the presentation. Imagine yourself taking a deep breath and diving right into the presentation. In your mind, repeat the entire speech as if you are really giving it. Practice answers for expected counter-arguments from your seniors. Visualize confidence in your stance and gestures. Don't forget to visualize the smile on your face.

When you have finished giving the presentation, imagine your seniors congratulating you on a job well done. Now, open your eyes, and let the feeling of confidence in your visualization course through your body. Repeat this visualization until your brain is rewired for self-assertiveness.

Meditation

When you meditate, you are connected with your thoughts and

emotions very deeply. This deep connection helps you discern between productive and unproductive thoughts. You can clearly see what went wrong in a particular situation, empowering you to handle them better in the future.

Meditation also helps you know the difference between aggression and assertiveness. You can fine-tune and alter your responses suitably when you realize this difference, thereby enhancing your level of self-awareness. With meditation comes calmness and peace which, in turn, empowers you to respond instead of reacting to difficult situations. You can use affirmations as mantras during your meditation sessions.

Maintaining a Diary
Make the following entries in your diary each day:
- The problems you experienced during the day.
- A suitable affirmation for each of the problems.
- Details of a mind-image for a better outcome than what you had.

For example, suppose your worst problem on a particular day was to get your project report all wrong. It was a mistake on your part, of course. However, your boss' reaction was quite rude and humiliating. You made the necessary corrections on the report, and the day finally ended.

Now, when you get home, write down three suitable affirmations for today's bad experience:
- My performance cannot be undermined by one correctable mistake.

- My boss' nasty reaction is a reflection of his nastiness and has nothing to do with me.
- Feeling bad and humiliated is a natural reaction, and I don't feel guilty or ashamed of it.

Next, visualize the same scene but imagine yourself standing up for your rights. For example, you could say, "Boss, I am sorry I made this mistake. However, it is a small and correctable one and does not really affect the overall picture. I don't believe it calls for a reaction that results in humiliation for me." While it might not make sense to speak like this in front of your colleagues, do visualize speaking to him in private, and letting him know that you were hurt by needless insults.

The Practice of Living with Purpose

NLP Techniques
A powerful NLP tool for living life purposefully is to set and follow SMART goals. SMART stands for:
S – Specific; for example, "By the end of this quarter, I will work hard and lose five pounds," is a specific and clear goal, unlike something as vague as "I will lose weight."
M – Measurable; In the above example, five pounds is measurable, whereas the second unspecific goal is not measurable; goals that do not have measurable aspects are not SMART goals.
A – Achievable; for example, "By the end of this quarter, I will work hard and lose five pounds," is an achievable goal, especially if you have a good weight-loss program ready to be

followed and implemented. However, "I will take over my boss' role by this quarter," is not achievable because it requires other uncontrollable factors to play a part.

R – Realistic; for example, losing five pounds in three months is highly realistic if you stick to your plans. However, setting a goal of losing thirty pounds in three months is highly unrealistic, and cannot be given the label of being a SMART goal. Instead, you must break down the thirty pounds into five-pound installments.

T – Time-bound; your goals must have an expiry date. For example, losing five pounds in three months is time-bound, whereas "I will lose weight" has no time limit, and therefore cannot be a SMART goal.

Affirmations
Use the following affirmations to live life purposefully:
- My entire being is infused with a deep sense of purpose.
- All my actions and choices are aligned with my purpose.
- As I connect deeply with my soul, my life's purpose becomes increasingly clear.
- I find my body and mind filled with joy and happiness as I live my life with purpose.
- Each day, my purpose gets clearer than before.
- Every choice I make and every action I take brings me closer to my purpose.

Visualization
Choose your life purpose first, and then use any of the visualization techniques to help you achieve your dreams and desires:

- Imagine the day when your coveted promotion is announced. Visualize yourself being greeted and congratulated by your colleagues, team members, and your boss. Feel the pride of receiving the much-awaited reward.
- Visualize yourself participating in a high-level corporate seminar, and making a big success of your presentation.
- Imagine looking at your bank statement with a big credit that is your bonus for the year. Don't hesitate to put a figure in your mind, and imagine the amount being credited to your account.
- Imagine yourself traveling the world and seeing beautiful places and writing about it in your blog.
- Visualize a happy home with the smells of cooking, the barking of a dog, the laughter of children, and other such beautiful things filling your home.

Powerful visualizations are great tools that effectively enhance your resolve and willpower to work hard and achieve your life's purpose.

Meditation
You need to continuously remind yourself of your life's purpose. Otherwise, it is bound to get lost in the din and noise of your daily routine. Your days are filled with work and activities that you hardly get time to spend with yourself, and in such a scenario, it is very easy to forget your life's purpose. In fact, if you don't keep track of your progress, you will see that your choices are counter-productive to your purpose.

Self Esteem For Women

Meditation is one of the best ways to keep reminding yourself of your life goals. As soon as you wake up, or before retiring to bed, sit for a few minutes in complete silence and solitude and repeat your life goal to yourself as a mantra or affirmation. For example, when the alarm wakes you up in the morning, don't jump out of bed immediately. Turn off the alarm, lie back on your bed, close your eyes, and repeat your life's purpose a couple of times. It could be anything, including:

- I promise to achieve my coveted promotion this year.
- I promise to work hard to earn more money to get myself that beautiful diamond ring.
- My life's purpose is to buy a beautiful home for my family.

Maintaining a Diary
You have already got your SMART goals in place by now. They are best recorded in your diary with sufficient space to make recordings of failed and successful milestones. Maintaining a diary is a great way to keep track of your progress and to know how much further you have to go before you achieve your life's purpose.

Maintaining a diary also keeps you alert and grounded. For example, suppose you have recently failed to achieve a particular milestone and are compelled to redo the effort. It is natural to feel discouraged and depressed during such difficult phases. Pick up your diary and read some of your success stories to feel motivated and rejuvenated.

Similarly, sometimes a string of successes can go to your head, and it is easy to let arrogance take control of your life. During such times, take a peek into your diary again, and reread the failures as a reminder to yourself that failure can come at any time during your life. Maintaining a diary, therefore, helps you to be grateful for your successes and the lessons learned from your failures.

The Practice of Personal Integrity

NLP Techniques
Personal integrity requires you to be true to your inner self. You practice what you preach and believe in. Leading a life of personal integrity requires a deep level of self-awareness regarding your values and principles. Some NLP tips to practice personal integrity:

-
- Don't be afraid to say no. Only then can you make those promises you can keep.
- Enhance your self-discipline so that you spend more time being productive rather than wasting time on valueless activities.
- Break down big goals into small, measurable, and timebound tasks for easy monitoring and ensuring that the final goal is reached in a systematic and disciplined way.

Affirmations
The following affirmations will help align your heart, mind, and

body with your core values, thereby allowing you to practice personal integrity throughout your life:
- Everything I say or do is a sincere promise.
- I value integrity and honesty above all else.
- I practice what I preach.
- I do not have a problem accepting my mistakes and learning from them.
- I always do the right thing, even in the face of unpopularity and dissension.
- I make only those promises that I can keep.

Visualization

Perform visualization techniques that reflect scenes in which you keep your promises and imagine the smiles on the faces of the positively-affected individuals. For example, suppose you promise to take your kids out for a weekend picnic and your boss then calls you into work. The choices you make in such situations reflect your level of personal integrity. Always think and make your choices.

Meditation

Meditation increases our self-awareness. Self-awareness helps us understand and appreciate our core values which, in turn, helps us practice personal integrity with greater intensity than before. Meditation allows you to get connected with the deepest parts of your mind and the reasons behind your current personality and state of life and why you believe in your chosen core values. This knowledge makes it easy for you to practice personal integrity.

Meditation also keeps your mind clear of useless, confusing, and unproductive thoughts. A calm and clear mind offers a strong foundation to practice personal integrity.

Maintaining a Diary
Maintaining a diary helps you keep track of the times when you end up breaking promises despite your best efforts. Whenever you have had to break a promise, either knowingly or unwittingly, make a note in your diary and keep reading these journal entries. Don't forget to include the description of the sad or upset faces of the affected people when you broke the promise, and your feeling of disappointment in yourself.

When a similar situation comes up in your life where you are on the brink of breaking a promise, go back and reread these instances. The description of the sadness and your disappointment will ensure you try and avoid a similar situation and will motivate you to keep your promise.

Chapter 5: Workbook

This workbook is aligned with the format of the six components explained with practical examples in Chapter 4. Completing the workbook requires a bit of time and effort. However, it will be worthwhile for you as the exercise will help you increase your self-awareness which, in turn, will help you increase your self-esteem slowly but surely. This workbook has a general outlook and can be used by anyone.

Before you attempt the workbook, you must complete the self-assessment quizzes and questions given in Chapter 2, which describes the six components of self-esteem in a bit of detail. Arrange the six components in increasing order of importance in your life. For example, if you believe that your current status in the practice of living purposefully is at the lowest level, start this workbook from that element.

Workbook for the Practice of Living Consciously

NLP Techniques – Focus on Your Thoughts
Before going to bed, make a note of the three most critical thoughts that occupied your mind today:

1) _____
_____
_____
_____
_____
_____

2) _____
_____
_____
_____
_____
_____

3) _____
_____
_____
_____
_____
_____

Self Esteem For Women

NLP Techniques – Prayers

At the end of every week, make a note of the three most crucial wishes that you want to come true in the coming week:

1)
_____
_____
_____
_____
_____
_____

2)
_____
_____
_____
_____
_____
_____

3)
_____
_____
_____
_____
_____
_____

Affirmations – Make a note of the three most vital affirmations aligned with your efforts to live consciously:

1)
_____

2) _____

3) _____

Visualization – Visualize the one most important goal that you want to achieve within a year, and make detailed notes, including:

The scene
_____

The people in it
_____

Smells
_____

Sounds
_____

Your feelings
_____

Self Esteem For Women

Meditation – When you complete your meditation session, what are the two most compelling thoughts that disturbed your meditation? Make a note of these two thoughts.

1) _____
_____
_____
_____
_____
_____

2) _____
_____
_____
_____
_____
_____

Maintaining a diary –Make a habit of reading your diary every week. Then, identify one element that was repeated at least twice for which you showed gratitude. If there was more than one, write all of them down:

1) _____
_____
_____
_____
_____
_____

Self Esteem For Women

Workbook for the Practice of Self-Acceptance

NLP anchoring technique - Take two of the most beautiful memories in your life. Create anchoring techniques for these experiences and practice them so that you can quickly retrieve them when needed.

1) _____
_____
_____
_____
_____

2) _____
_____
_____
_____
_____

Affirmations – Think for yourself and make a note of three affirmations for self-acceptance:

1) _____
_____

2) _____
_____

3) _____
_____

Visualization – Can you imagine yourself happy? Write a detailed scene of one such happy moment in your life.
_____
_____
_____
_____
_____
_____

Meditation – Meditate on any of the affirmations for self-acceptance that you created for yourself. Alternately, you can use one of the following:
- I love myself unconditionally
- I accept my weaknesses with humility and my strengths with joy

Workbook for the Practice of Self-Responsibility

The NLP Swish technique – What are the three most painful unwanted triggers? Identify replacement triggers for each of them:
Unwanted trigger 1)
_____
_____

Replacement trigger 1)
_____
_____

Unwanted trigger 2)
_____
_____

Replacement trigger 2)
_____
_____

Unwanted trigger 3)
_____
_____

Replacement trigger 3)
_____
_____

Affirmation – Write three self-responsibility affirmations of your own.
1)
_____
_____

2)_____
_____

3)_____
_____

Visualization – Think of the most important goal of your life. Now, imagine the day you will achieve it. Make detailed notes of this visualization.

Self Esteem For Women

_____
_____
_____
_____
_____
_____

Meditation – Recall a painful event in your life. Relive the experience, minus the attached emotions, and write down the various reasons for it. Make two categories of the contributing factors:

Under your control

_____
_____
_____
_____
_____
_____

Not under your control

_____
_____
_____
_____
_____
_____

Workbook for the Practice of Self-Assertiveness
NLP techniques – Look at the following example questions and answer honestly:

Self Esteem For Women

If you had to make a choice between going to a party and completing your project report, due tomorrow, which would you choose? Why?

If you have to choose between a boring but honest and upright man and a handsome and dashing man who is a liar and cheater, who will you choose and why?

Affirmations – Complete the following self-assertiveness affirmations in your own words:

1) I am
_____
_____

2) I am not deterred by
_____
_____

3) I stand up for
_____
_____

Visualization – Recall a particularly difficult situation that keeps recurring in your life in which you find it tough to say no. Now, visualize this situation in your mind and imagine confidently saying no. Make detailed notes of your imagination including the choice of words, body language, gestures, tone of voice, etc.
_____
_____

Self Esteem For Women

_____
_____
_____
_____

Workbook for the Practice of Living With Purpose

NLP techniques – Write down three of your most important life goals, ensuring all of them fulfill the SMART goal requirement:
- S – Specific
- M – Measurable
- A – Achievable
- R – Realistic
- T – Timebound

Affirmations – Write down three affirmations that are aligned with your life's purpose:

1) _____
_____

2) _____
_____

3) _____
_____

Visualization – Rate the following goals in order of the importance in your life:
- Completing an advanced course that will help in boosting

your career
- Getting a promotion
- Earning lots of money
- Traveling the world
- Following a favorite hobby

Now, for the first three goals, imagine you have achieved the successful outcome as per your desires. Write down the visuals in detail. Don't hesitate to make your own goals if none of the above match your desires.

Workbook for the Practice of Personal Integrity
NLP techniques – Look at the following examples of how to say no politely. Practice them regularly. In fact, you can use them as affirmations for daily practice. Remember the importance of learning to say no to ensure you make only those promises you can keep.
- I am afraid this is not a good fit for me
- Sounds very interesting, but at present I'm really pressed for time
- I am sorry, but I have to pass up your invitation this time.
- If I agree to help you simply because you are insisting on it, I will be making a false promise
- Sorry, this does not fit my present schedule

Affirmations – Create three affirmations for personal integrity:

1)
_____
_____

Self Esteem For Women

2)
_____
_____

3)
_____
_____

Meditation – Use all of the above affirmations to meditate on daily.

Maintaining a diary – Think of two of the most difficult times in your life when you broke promises to people you loved and cared for. Now, answer the following questions:
Why did you break the promise?
_____
_____
_____
_____

What were your feelings?
_____
_____
_____
_____

What were the lessons you learned which helped you improve your personal integrity?
_____

Self Esteem For Women

Chapter 6: Conclusion

Lisa Lieberman-Wang, the famous author of many self-help books, says, *"You are not your mistakes; they are what you did, not who you are."*

Building self-esteem is not an overnight exercise. It takes time and sustained efforts to build your self-esteem slowly and steadily. It is important for you to first make the decision to change yourself for the better. This crucial decision is the start of a long but fun journey. Don't worry if you initially face failures. Stumbling on the way is the best way to make your learning effective.

Continue to increase your self-awareness about the six components of self-esteem discussed in this book. Repeat the quizzes and questionnaires given here to keep track of your progress. The journey of building self-esteem may seem long and arduous, especially if you are a victim of low self-esteem. Don't be discouraged by the challenges you will encounter. Simply continue to persist, and make the development of the base components of self-esteem discussed in this book a lifelong effort.

Self Esteem For Women

This book is specifically targeted at women with low self-esteem. The self-assessment exercises and templates given in this book are extremely useful to accurately gauge your current status, and then to build efficient plans to develop self-esteem.

Confidence, self-esteem, and assertiveness are all related and yet different from each other. The main focus of this book was on Self Esteem.

Read the other books *for women* from Maria van Noord:
- Confidence for Women
- Assertiveness for Women

24939128R00045

Printed in Great Britain
by Amazon